1

The Enigma

Considering the state of our world, I believe we can agree that God's actual presence is not here within the physical dimension. His absence is more than noticeable by the turmoil and negativity evident in most places. It's a time when there appears to be so much available on a physical level for some and others almost nothing when the world of spiritual awareness has virtually faded from sight.

Physical and material supports have indeed proliferated, yet the qualities needed to experience and enjoy such profusion have yet to. Many are stuck on the empty roundabout of accumulation, others are tremulous with fear of losing what little they have, and others are just in a desperate state of yearning for what others have.

This nowhere misery route marks an

important and pivotal point for our world. In this spiritual darkness, we are all affected; we are all, in one way or another, beginning to search and reach out, consciously or unconsciously, for more meaningful and subtle ways to find an alternative form of support and experience.

These manifestations are an indication of a coming change, a new attitude to life, a changing of consciousness, and a questioning of our formerly narrow and over-programmed physicalised existence.

Many are now querying and rejecting consumerism's mind-killing, soul-killing anthems of need and accumulation, a never-fulfilling, never-ending process of more!

Many may be asking, what is God doing during all this turmoil? Watching, ignoring or having just given up on us?
God is probably the most adored, praised, reviled, abused, and possibly blamed in human history.

Called the Creator and yet, labelled as the one who brings things to an end. God is said to be everywhere and nowhere. He has unlimited compassion and yet, apparently, seems indifferent to what is going on. In many beliefs, He is the one who says, have love for one and all, yet declares I am your only genuine beloved.

In many teachings, it is encouraged to invoke such a Divine personality to resolve, solve and finish all sorrows to bring happiness and harmony and by others, He is seen as an appendage of control and suppression and is thus rejected. And for many, God is a being for the superstitious, a figure of historical fantasy, and so is disregarded or wholly ignored.

A dichotomy, a paradox of all paradoxes.

Can it be possible to make sense of such a conundrum? A personality about which everyone, it seems, has an opinion and view

It might seem to many very presumptuous to be trying to write anything about God, the limited trying to grasp the unlimited, a Being that is considered beyond the ability of the human mind to attempt to comprehend. An attempt that many would even consider sacrilegious or an act that would end up eventually twisted and defamatory.

I would concur with some of these statements; to veer into idle speculation, jumping from one supposition to another would end in a frustrating cul-de-sac, arriving nowhere, having gone nowhere.

I believe using the physical mind to try and gain a deeper understanding of God's nature is nearly impossible. However, this writer, working with the knowledge that God is a nonphysical being, has tried to position himself in a similar mode of spiritual synchronicity, allowing the mind to liaise, link and think on an equal frequency of mutual receptivity, awareness and touching.

2

Interpretation

In most beliefs, God is considered an all-knowing, powerful, pure, and benign personality.

And amongst them, there is a strong belief that we all are, in some way, God or that we are part of Him or He is part of us.

Yet, with all our foibles, weaknesses, desires and confusions, this unfolding list of negativities quickly dispels this notion that we are this perfected Being, wouldn't you agree? However, the vast amount of so-called suppositions and statements concerning God's existence and nature possibly suggests that humanity, in the past, has previously had some connection and experience with God and His teachings. Strangely this could be the seed of our delusions, a distorted ego memory, believing solely in the supremacy of itself as this Divine being.

However, what is the reality of this world of

many "Gods?"

Mistakes, wrong choices, and being embroiled in issues and disagreements. Each desiring this or that, feeling empty and needy and everywhere stress and upheaval, causing numerous breakdowns in individuals, families and relationships.

And all the while, the world is falling apart from divisions, terrorism, economic mismanagement, planetary abuse, and the occasional local war.

How could all this happen when each is or part of this Divine being called God?
Yet, the mind is now so confused and befuddled that it soon begins to believe it is this highest Being of spiritual divinity, so it's no wonder the being of God is ridiculed or rejected. The conflicting pronouncements from the numerous religions and scriptural writings add to the confusion.

Each philosophical belief is structured and organised around the perceptions and teachings of its particular founder. And so, each in their unique way declares that God is this, is not that, does this, but not that, can be reached here, but not there, and so on.

Then, after the founder's departure, the close followers validate the original beliefs and add further to the interpretation of God by throwing in their views and personal insights. More ingredients to the mix come from the many followers who come after these, adding more of their views and perceptions.

Eventually, a system, a way, a recognisable set of teachings is established that demands to be believed and followed.

The teachings and beliefs are further embedded as they gain increasing adherents, all believing so and saying so, primarily because they were told it was so by those before them.

The belief system then formulates as something extraordinary, eternal, and absolute, emanating, as it is usually claimed, from the divine, infallible perceptions and interpretations of various individuals who either stated they were God, were sent from God, or were inspired by God.

Each belief is never the same or in concurrence with those of other ways, yes, occasionally in alignment about certain things, like values and behaviours, but mostly giving differing views, especially about the nature and role of God.

So, we end up like the proverbial blind men trying to make sense of the elephant. Their judgement is based on their limited use of what they can only touch.

So, this seepage of subtle memory and the influences of the past thoughts of others have led us to this state of partial insight, which in turn has given rise to the jumble of mixed truths and ideas we have been used to hearing and accepting.

So, we end up in a web of illogical positions, in an almost comic book game of an implausible and ludicrous set of situations, characters and narratives. And all the while, the quagmire of illusion and falsehood is added to by the chaotic masquerades of the increasing God-like stand-ins.

A few hang in and blindly follow, but it seems there is an ever-increasing disillusionment with these beliefs in God and the many affiliated ways to a promised land of harmony and happiness for many others. For these, there needs to be more return and more experience.

Thus, for many, God is now seen mainly as a

mythological and, maybe, a non-existent and irrelevant being.

3

New Ways

In recent years there has been a massive increase and explosion of materialism and materialistic ways. Never in our history has there been such a proliferation of things, and together with this, a clarion call to accumulate, to possess these things.

This bombardment, it seems, has obsessed the human mind, and in acceding to these ways, it has been overwhelmed by the accompanying flood of things and choices Ancient tales talk of a loss of a former paradisal state through a universal flood.

To my mind, this flood is this consumerist tsunami which has swallowed and submerged our spiritual nature and, with it, the memory of God.

Interestingly, at this same time, there appears for many a lack of inner fulfilment and deep dissatisfaction with what now seems the empty promises of materialism's so-called golden worlds of happiness and contentment. With vast outlays on property, cars, jewelry and escapist holidays and activities, many are now discovering these are not bringing the euphoric joy, and personal bliss promised as part of the deal.

A part of this revival and interest has been in revisiting God as a being and a way to some solution. However, this area has been blended into the concepts of omnipresence, and universal oneness -a return to insanity, I believe, via the back door. Yet, still, many have been motivated and influenced to find an alternative lifestyle, to take a different direction, one that is more meaningful and fulfilling.

4

Aspiration

The history of religious practice tells us of the many routes and rites to try and connect and communicate with God.

Throughout time, prayer and associated acts of supplication have been the primary vehicles used to try and achieve this social/ spiritual state of well-being and become the main avenue to reach God to entice Him to help and restore the World to some order.

Interestingly, in prayer, using focused and positive thought, a subtle and uplifting resonance can be experienced from the self's deeper consciousness, which is a storehouse of all higher experiences. The prayer experience can cause a release of these positive energies allowing the supplicant to feel uplifted, creating a lightness and a sense of well-being; the devotee then feels their prayers are being answered.

However, these feelings, I believe, are not from

a connection with God but from the qualities within the soul itself, part of its original nature.

Though devotees would probably disagree, most would be philosophically caught between the beliefs of an external Divinity and a divinity within. Though most would just be happy to have an experience of a listening, caring God. For them, this is what matters.

In the practice of hatha yoga, there is no real connection with God in any form or way. It's a practice that uses the body's physicality to divert the conscious mind away from its immediate connections and relationship with its body to achieve its goals. Indeed, in its practice, there can be some relief for the mind, and physical benefit for the body experienced.

In this process, the mind is shifting its focus temporarily away from its body, so it feels a sense of release and well-being. Though, it's a bit like a prisoner looking from his cell window thinking he has been given freedom.

In today's material world, the general belief that achievement and success will only arise when we do something physical has infiltrated into the realms of spirituality, such as through praying, singing of hymns, readings, donations, fasting and pilgrimage and so on. These have become part of the so-called necessary, almost obsessional, criteria needed to enter the world of God.

So, through all these activities, are we somehow hinting that God is unaware or oblivious to our wants, and so we try to get God to notice us or wake Him up to our needs and circumstances?

It's probably safe to say that God is certainly not a recluse or shy in making Himself available or coming forward to help. However, we are so often in a state that prevents us from receiving help, too often fixated and trapped by imposed religious practices and philosophies, too often blindsided by our accumulated fears and increasing needs, that we find ourselves entrenched in a smothering web of negative thinking and materialistic experiences, that do not allow the subtle, sacred, silent power of God to reach us.

5

Resolution

So, do we follow the voice of our spiritual heart, or do we yield to our old ways and fears and either return to a half-hearted form of devotion or the glitzy glamour and allure of materialism?

To resolve our spiritual quandary, we need a subtle and spiritual approach. We must step back from the polarities that stand before us and ask our spiritual heart what both worlds are saying and where they are taking us. Does their way bring me a feeling of fulfilment and contentment or much of the same old disillusionment?

When we step back before decision-making, we can use reflective awareness to grasp the bigger picture and see things less emotionally and more clearly. This kind of analysis works when we come to these crossroads with a pure and honest attitude, especially to re-discover our way back to God's essential Being. As we link with this pure consciousness, we open a doorway, a release catch on our former inability to see through the hazy fumes of our fears and illusions.

It's then that God's vibrational energy support becomes evident and usable. As we engage with this power, we strengthen our nascent faith and growing spiritual memory; with this renewed enthusiasm and growing purpose, we can move forward.

The process of connecting or communing with God can be called yoga. Yoga means connecting the physical mind or thoughts to the Divine mind's subtle form and energy body.

A better self and world will manifest through that union of energies. For this to happen, one must be clear about what is occurring. We need to know to whom we are linking and what should be our actual focus.

Our meditation concentrates on unifying with God's power. To help us, we can visualise God's being or form as a non-physical, pure spiritual energy, an eternal, perfect point of resonant light.

Adopting a similar form and attitude would be necessary for the mind to benefit from this fusion with God's pure consciousness. In doing so, we can experience an incredible inflow and transmission of the most refined spiritual power.

For this to be effective, by holding in our awareness our soul form of spiritual light, with this stability and power, we can link and keep our mind within the unlimited centre of God's pure Being, a vast spiritual energy, which, like a spiritual sun is constantly radiant, benevolent and powerful; an energy of awareness, an energy form of love. And just as the Sun regenerates our physical world, so by linking with the highest spiritual power of God, there is a restoration of the mind's depleted soul energy, manifesting primarily through its central qualities of peace and love.

In this union, there is a renewing, a restoring of the self's spiritual nature, a harmonisation with the energy fields of the physical worlds and the discovery and realignment with God, the source of pure energy and spiritual power.

6

Discovery

God, a being of perfect vibrational energy, would not be found or located within the sphere of our physical world, subject as it is to entropy and, with it, the gradual disintegration of all pure forms.

So thus, God would indeed be outside this domain of change, being Himself unchanging, constant and beyond all corrupting energies. Or, as portrayed on film, TV and popular pulp, possibly found dwelling in some Heavenly realm? However, being non-physical and wholly fulfilled, God would not need to experience these mythical lands of many delights.

As much as mythology and scriptural fairy tales try to place Him in some fabulous and heroic form, we have managed to conclude that God has no physical form; that is, He is incorporeal and remains so, as we've mentioned, He doesn't take birth, for to do so, being lawful, would cause Him to have to comply with the laws of karma and all the comings and goings of the play of life that happens on the physical plane, including also, the fact, He would have to live and thus, also have to die.

Yet, beyond all the ideas and conjecture about God's Being and whereabouts, what is consistent is that in most beliefs, is an awareness that He can somehow untangle and resolve our confusions. From this, we can deduce that God is a benevolent and beneficial being whose nature is to help, resolve and heal.

So, we set out to find Him and get Him back to sort things out!

Shall we experiment and connect to the light form, love energy centre of this Divine Being and experience this long sort-after help?

> *I am a subtle, light form of energy,*
> *My nature, my natural state, is light,*
> *I hold and experience this thought and this experience.*
>
> *This now gives me the ability to take my mind*
> *To a region, a dimension beyond the physical world, and there connect with*

the radiant energy of God's great love,
Centred in that vibrant light, form energy,
My thoughts are drawn, absorbed
By that pure form, that pure energy,
I am held in that light,
I am surrounded emersed in that pure love, light energy,
There is nothing but light and increasing light.
I am energised,
Empowered by that great purity,
That great Light.
So, I stay in this experience, in this unity.

In this experience, our focus and connection are with God's light form and energetic body of spiritual power. His pure energy reignites our dormant spiritual soul. His light touches our light, and there is an immediate rejuvenation within our consciousness. We emerge from the hidden shadowlands of unawareness and non-experience, totally empowered.

Through this inner experience, through this journey of change and transformation, we view ourselves with spiritual insight and gain a deeper understanding and awareness of the nature and being of God, which becomes more apparent and more evident through each subsequent connection.

In meditation, the transmittance of God's pure light diffuses itself into the soul's primal powers, formulating the light of love, peace, and awareness. It's renewing the soul's innate nature, enabling a return to its pure and original state.

Such is the empowerment from the connection with God's vast energy; the individual mind quickly rises above the influences of its former negativities and suppressive illusions and naturally unites with its long-forgotten spiritual nature.

The challenge for us at this point is to hold and embed this newly awakened awareness and prevent it from slipping away, so meditation becomes the means to help instruct the subconscious mind into accepting and welcoming this new identity.

Using the following thoughts, let's reaffirm this spiritual understanding for our reunification of consciousness.

> *I am a spiritual being,*
> *Needing now to rejuvenate my spiritual nature,*
> *Increasing my inner strength of patience,*

acceptance and cooperation
Emerging my natural qualities of love,
compassion and peace.
I now connect to God's central source of power,
My light becomes filled with that light,
A great wave of love pulses through my being,
Renewal and transformation begin,
I hold this experience,
Feel it, become it,
I am this power,
I become this power,
I am combined,
In the unity of God's marvelous light.

Through the practice of affirmation, we can allow ourselves to accept these truths, experience them and allow them to be integrated into our spiritual world. Repeating these affirmations with awareness and love, they gradually become our nature and part of our being.

In these initial stages of experience, God empowers the individual to realise that the soul is a spiritual, eternal, and self-existent being. And as these new life energies of the soul begin to flow through the arteries of consciousness, the soul soon realises its spirituality and eternal uniqueness and that

God is enabling this rebirth of awareness, facilitating this process of self-realisation. This precious new awareness is the first step in the journey back to self-regeneration, bringing healing, harmony, and the feeling that God is once more the Companion of the soul.

As wonderful as this experience is, it can be a tremendous shock to many that the world of God-conscious spirituality is opposite to their previously held materialistic beliefs that proclaimed satisfaction and happiness can only come from a world of accumulation and form. Spirituality now tells us what we need and have been searching for, has been with us all the while; it is within us and part of the soul itself, and now, through God's support and help, we can regain and experience these inner treasures once again.

With this changing and reassembling, old mindsets and attitudes can often resurface, echoing fears and anxieties about what might be lost, what others might say, and whether I am doing the right thing.

These forming fears can be allayed by reminding ourselves about what we are changing and what we are gaining. By moving into silence, these voices from the past quickly fade, and we can again reconnect with our pure intention through the affirmation:

> *I am light*
> *Linked to God's incredible light,*
> *And this pure light emerges my inner world of fullness and fulfilment,*
> *There are now no more needs, no more desires,*
> *I see the illusions, the false masks and the empty promises*
> *I am full of God's great power*
> *I now have all I need*

An area to think about is the use of the word God. It has overtones generally of a distant being, a being beyond knowing, one to respect, fear, or have a love for, a term that we use so that we can call on when needed. Though unfortunately, in recent times, it has become a throw-away term, even used as an expletive, such has God's presence and memory so fallen and been forgotten.

As we have already seen, when we adopt an attitude of subtle spirituality, God's formerly vast and unknown personality begins to be discovered. It's then that we can move away from our old attitudes and feelings aligned with the past and now can use the term God with an understanding and respect connected with His actual role and state of Being.

This rethinking of the term God will significantly help us in our ability to connect in our yoga meditation. It will help to change our former devotional attitudes and mindsets, so long conditioned by such feelings of being insignificant and unworthy and help escape the blocks of a fearful judgementalism and punishment from "God's right hand."

So, as we reflect more on God's qualities and His role as a caring and benevolent being who can be a source of change and hope, He becomes more approachable, a means of direct support and renewal. Also, using more familiar and loving names like Beloved, Divine, the Highest Being, Mother, and even Friend, our connection deepens, and we start to come closer. It's about choosing whatever feels suitable for us.

Our old and often disillusioned religious attitudes and feelings that God can only be accessed via the help of some intermediary quickly dissipate as we connect directly and are open to God's loving and uplifting energies.

In meditation, we can now directly experience God's empathic love vibrations, which begin to wash, soothe and irradiate our entire being. An incredible long sought-after power is now brought into our newly awakened consciousness.

The depletion of energies through entropy is arrested, and the mind is now taken into an elevated vortex of pure spiritual power.
This new realignment with God is like bringing Him into being, back again into our lives, back again from non-existence. (To use Him or She implies a gender, a physical being, however, for the convenience of language, I will use Him.)

Thus, previously long lost and long forgotten amongst the swathes of confused conjecture and maze of scriptural directions, in discovering God as our support and main guide for our life's eternal journey, it now becomes relatively easy to abandon our beliefs in the artificial gods of a quick consumerist fix and immediate return.

Through our ongoing meditation practice, we will still have to deal with the resurgence from time to time of our old false natures, which are often triggered by the sounds and structures of a still very active world of illusions.

Like an awakening dragon, they raise their heads and open their eyes but slip back to their illusory depths with no engagement.

7

Manifestation

On life's grand stage, we see an ever-increasing unhappy and chaotic world, causing many naturally to ask, what is God doing in all of this? Can He help us?
God would, of course, be aware of what is happening and what solutions are needed. I believe responding dramatically is not His way like a wizard with a magic wand to make everything right.

At every turn, something or someone seems linked to a wrong choice of actions or a wrong set of desires—the result of either a lack of awareness or an emotionally damaging nature.
Of course, some short-term intervention by God would undoubtedly ease things, yet, inevitably, as the seed of the actions is not being directly addressed, the situations would emerge again in some form or another.

So, God being aware of this causative law, comes not as a Gandalf figure but as a teacher, enabling us to see where we went wrong and giving us the necessary powers and qualities to respond positively and correctly, so creating in us a nature of correct behaviour for future times. So, what happens is that as the mind opens itself to the experience of the higher consciousness of God and as a result, old nature and old attitudes gradually become displaced. The soul's original nature, its innate spiritual nature, reasserts itself.

Without God's influential body of pure spiritual power, the individual human mind, I believe, would certainly not have the strength or the capability to effect this inner transformation. The overwhelming combined effects of a negative and entrenched physical personality and an ingrained and confused belief system, all compacted by a surrounding world atmosphere of fear and greed, are much too strong for the mind by itself to break free and reach clear water.

The entry of God into this scenario is like sunlight breaking through the storm-laden clouds on a dark winter's day; everything changes.

Many will ask, so why don't all benefit from this powerful and beneficial energy? All do so, but in differing ways according to their choices and levels of receptivity.

God's help and support are not an enforced experience but more about individual choices and decisions. Some prefer to stay with their idea of God or Gods, whether in the forms of created images, individuals or something from the natural world. Others, having a fear of change or being wary of any imposed system, thus, remain with what they have.

The Sun may be shining, yet some decide to stay inside, in the shadowlands of old attitudes, unwilling or lacking the courage to step into the open light of new experiences and let go of their fears and harmful attachments. Ones who take benefit often try to help their fellows, calling, knocking, shouting even through the letter box....it's OK, you'll enjoy, you can be helped, it's great! But alas, no one answers or comes to the door (probably hoping they'll soon go away!)....and so it is.

Our world is a forum of many beliefs; many are content with what they have and happy with what they've been told.

However, most beliefs now have little strength and power during this time of extreme entropy. So, the followers often need more inner capacity to use their received teachings. However, God offers His help and understanding to the troubled soul at this time, providing an opportunity to regenerate and recover through the infusion of pure direct energy and the chance to move into a more significant state of knowing.

So let us connect and make sense of this through the inner journey of unity,

> *With the awareness of my spiritual nature,*
> *I emerge my form of light,*
> *I become that light*
> *And in this subtle form of spiritual light,*
> *I open my spiritual heart,*
> *To the love centre of God's pure form,*
> *And waves upon waves of light energy love,*
> *Surround and draw me,*
> *Pull me deep into the absolute world of God's pure being,*
> *I am no more,*
> *I have no feeling of self,*
> *No awareness of form,*
> *Or the worlds around,*
> *I am with God,*
> *We have merged, come together,*
> *And I am held,*
> *Centred in that subtle energy of perfect*

form,
A consciousness not tangible or definable,
With no boundaries,
Infinite and unlimited,
Here love centred,
My soul becomes this
And is perfectly still,
For there is only love.

8

Questions to God

Many people dream of meeting God, so in my dream meeting, I ask what we all might ask personally or would surely ask in our meditations.

Q. Do you have a personality like us?

When you take birth, the coming together of the influences of your body, your role, your emerging nature and the interaction with the outside world formulates your personality.
I do not take birth. I am and remain a spiritual being.

Q. So, what do you think about what goes on in your mind?

I do not think. My mind is of stillness.
The physical mind of man is in a constant state of thinking as it interacts with life's everchanging world, organising, analysing, reconciling and responding to the battery of influences and external effects. All the time is

trying to make sense of what it perceives.
I hold the cycle of your time constantly in my awareness. Knowing what was, what is and what is to be. I do not need to deliberate. I know. I do not need to think.

Q. Other than God, do you have a name?

A name is a bodily label connecting with the part the soul plays. As I do not have a body, I have no name. I do have a role of giving and benevolence. It is one of bringing help and benefit. You can use terms that describe this role, such as Benefactor, Teacher, Mother, etc. You are familiar with many such descriptions.

Q. So, where do you come from?

I reside in a dimension beyond form, beyond change and beyond experience, in a location that resonates with my consciousness, created by my consciousness. It is a place beyond the descriptive limitations of language and your present capacity of awareness. To help grasp it, you can call it the land beyond or Nirvana, a region beyond everything.

Q. Are you always here, or do you come at a particular time?

The play of life involves human souls

interacting and playing their roles, making sense of what they have and what they understand—learning through positive actions and developing awareness and understanding to use in activities and parts that follow.
I have no role at that time. I come when complete awareness has been lost and confusion rampant. When needed, I help the human soul return to its truth and original spiritual nature in whatever form that each would recognise.

Q. Do you at any time take a human birth?

I can pose a question to you, why would I need to incarnate? Why would I place such a vast consciousness in such a limited form? What would that achieve?

The physical bodies that souls adopt enable them to discover and experience the satisfaction and contentment of their original spiritual nature and eternal truth, together with the experience of the happiness and harmony of an ordered and paradisal world. I do not need to experience Myself, as I am beyond experience and completely self-realised.

Q. What happens when the body dies?

Each soul is involved in the great drama of life. As in a play, the actors are not the parts they are playing, so in the same way, a soul, who uses a body costume to play particular roles, will always remain a soul but never becomes those parts. A role finishes, the soul moves into another situation, another set of relationships, and its former body reformulates back into the energy field of matter.

As the three main players of this drama, soul, God and matter are all eternal energies, nothing finishes, and nothing ends; thus, there is no death, only change, which occurs only to all material forms. The soul does not change; it just changes the costume of the body. God is constant and unchanging.
All roles and all scenes of the play of life are influenced by what has gone before. This is called karma, or cause and effect and will determine the type of role and the interactions to follow.

This is called rebirth, or the evolution of the soul's journey through time.

Q. Do you punish souls for their wrongdoings?

I am a being of love. My form and spiritual nature are of love; I cannot cause or give sorrow. When a soul plays its role without awareness and love, it can often come under influence, and its actions may cause suffering. When a soul leaves its body, it can experience fear of the unknown, again creating great anxiety and dread, becoming fearful of the repercussions of what it did or did not do in its previous birth. Also, a soul brings memories and resonances of prior interactions while in the womb. As a result, it will often experience sorrow and regret for its former action.

Q. How do you help us?

The way of help and transformation is achieved through the intellect, the mind's primary port of receptivity and union. Receiving the vibrational support from God in meditation, the intellect becomes the hub of this regeneration process by channeling pure, transformative, light energy to all the essential workings of consciousness.

The intellect is the heart of being. The more it opens to its spiritual experiences and ponders on significance and connectivity the more there is a stirring, an awakening in the mind's wisdom centre.

In these first steps of meditation, the mind is aided by the constant encouragement and support of God's energy and love.

Initially, this interaction is in the form of subtle guidance and inspiration, through which the soul learns about its reality and how it should take personal responsibility for restoring the imbalances that have occurred. The impact on the mind of this connection is such that it awakens the soul's spiritual consciousness, which then can allow God's healing love into its hurt and fragmented heart.

Q. So what is Meditation?

Meditation is the coming together, the union of soul and God; it is the combining of both these spiritual energies. The former crippled mind is supported and guided by God into the arena of pure thought and spiritual freedom, where it gradually develops a greater sense of spiritual self-realisation. In experiencing its emerging spiritual qualities, the mind can quickly finish its former sorrows and weaknesses. It can relinquish its attachments and allegiances to a past of false philosophy and lifestyle. This clarity and power then provide it with the ability to have a deeper understanding of God's nature and so be able to gain a new strength to help in its ongoing life journey.

Now in an empowered and elevated state, the mind, like a fragile forming butterfly, finds itself delicately poised between its former antagonistic world and a new and welcoming subtle state of pure vibrational light, which it now naturally and easily embraces.

Q. Can you tell me more about what is happening in Meditation?

Meditation is the coming together of the souls emerging spiritual memories and inner spiritual powers with God's unlimited awareness world.

Through introversion, the soul enters the inner dimension of silence. Understanding its energy form, it can become and align with this light body. The soul is then helped and drawn into God's pure protective light energy field. Here it can become focused and centred, so staying beyond the contaminated lower energy fields, whose effect would soon cause the newly installed spiritual light to all too quickly dissipate and disappear and so with this connection, it can reinforce the change that is developing.

Here power is filled, two forms, two energies, separate, becoming as one. The souls, once diminishing strength, is immediately arrested and begin regenerating.

The pure and infinite light of the Supreme holds the mind in its auric field, and as the connection stabilises, the soul's spiritual state soon starts to appear as a recognisable reality. Maintaining this link, the soul begins to experience these higher light energies more profoundly, so reviving the fading qualities of its pure nature, which activated and empowered, now emerge rising to the surface of waking awareness.

Now freed and healed, the soul begins its dance of inner joy. Its old impure consciousness and attitude dissolve in the upsurge of this renewed spiritual power, enabling the soul to move into clarity and acceptance. So, it can more knowingly cooperate with its spiritual change.

Q. How does Meditation affect us Individually?

As it begins to master the meditation process, the soul's revived spiritual energies manifest and work in three main ways.

On a personal level, they fill the soul with the natural nourishment of spiritual well-being. Meditation makes the soul's spiritual qualities evident and available to use in every situation. They ignite awareness and understanding and become a mirror, a trigger, a reminder and an example for others of their spiritual nature.

On a subtle level, the unified energies of the soul and God combine to create a spiritual resonance to awaken, touch and inspire souls to discover and experience their own higher consciousness.

On a vibrational level, the mind becomes a sounding board, a transmitter to lift and change the negative frequencies of matter and individuals overwhelmed by the illusions of a non-spiritual world, helping to change these and the surrounding atmospheres.

So, the mind empowered by God now experiences itself to be in a state of spiritual freedom, a state beyond the influences of its old, programmed ego, beyond the control and restrictions of the non-benevolent worlds, for now, it can determine its destiny, create its momentum, and move forward in whatever direction it chooses.

Q. What is the Purpose of Meditation, this

coming together with You?

As we have seen, the soul, through time, has fallen into an illusory dream state of forgetfulness due to the attraction of form and artificial spirituality, a windowless prison of spiritual unconsciousness. Thus, turning away from God loses contact with the source of truth, power and spiritual sustenance. In frustration, humanity destroys itself through anger, greed and selfishness.

Then it becomes God's role to put right these things that have gone so badly wrong. To reveal the right ways, to heal, unify and set the laws of correct living and lifestyle again, and to reassert the world of truth once more. So, God enters the drama of life and shows a way out of this predicament by igniting the soul's spiritual memory through meditation, allowing it to restore the worlds of harmony and order.

Q. What about those who do not meet you or those from other beliefs? How are they helped, and to what level?

Not all souls have and desire such a direct connection. Many receive guidance and support according to their needs, beliefs and personal efforts, which would come through different and indirect agencies.

The members of differing belief systems would rely on the dissemination of God's guidance and support processes through their founder or close interpreters of their particular philosophy.

Not having a direct link, the impact and effect would be by the spiritual stance of those sharing these spiritual teachings. However, the purity and the effect of the initial sharing, now with so many additions, would not have the strength of its original form.

Q. What are you feeling when you see what's happening in the world? What are you doing?

I am where I am, beyond, in a state of constant bliss. I am not involved in the world of change and fluctuating energies. I am not affected or influenced by the collective dramas being played below. I am not affected by the chaos and turmoil, the protestations, the imploring and the whole litany of needs and attempts that try to pull me into some response and action.

It is a play, a game, where souls conform to their parts, to the play of life. And all the forthcoming complaining, calling and blaming are also part of the play because souls have forgotten it is just a play.

So, I watch this play until the time comes for me to go and remind the players of the game's rules; thus, harmony and order can once again be restored.

Q. How does Meditation Affect and Influence Our World?

Through the continued practice of the link between the mind and the mind of God, the soul moves into the highest and most elevated level of purity and spiritual awareness, transforming its attitude and vibrational frequency.

This has a tremendous repercussive effect on the energy fields of the planet, which are reactive and receptive; the impact and the change are dramatic and beneficial. Energies that were once chaotic and frenetic, vibrating and manifesting at a very low frequency, are now imbued and uplifted by the pure love-channeled energies of the Divine.

All forms, all beings, and everything on the planet are influenced; an incredible metamorphosis occurs. The world changes. All has shifted into the unlimited.

In this unity of combined Soul and God, there comes a tipping point for the individual soul, where purity's balance moves, shifts, and becomes the dominant effect. This sets an auto-synchronicity connecting all energy systems, especially for those directly involved in this renewal.

Nature, the animal kingdoms and all forms of the material world comply and naturally become part of this vast spiritual transformation, all becoming part of this elevated world community of spiritual harmony.

Q. Since you are God, can't You make things happen to move all into a unity that will bring renewal and well-being for the whole planet?

Indeed, if souls are willing and ready to let go of the things blocking and hindering the incoming higher spiritual energies.
Adapting to this particular course of action, where all are brought on board, brings up the issue of free will and the choice to do what each wants and to experience what each one desires.
Many have no desire to relinquish their hold

on their physical trophies or let go of their infatuation with form and the experiences of the physical world.

Yet, entry to this spiritual dimension is available for those who wish for a more subtle and elevated lifestyle and to experience a higher state of consciousness.

To allow the pure energies of God to be experienced, the mind of the receiver has to let go of the old contaminants of impure relationships, lifestyle and behaviour that formerly took the mind into spirals of reactive thinking and vibration; otherwise, nothing will take hold, and all will slip away, as the influences of physicality would quickly start to reassert themselves once again.

Q. What one piece of advice would you give now to humanity?

At this time when energy systems are significantly degraded and dissipating and souls now need a great deal of support and reassurance, having an attitude of good wishes and pure feelings for whatever now occurs or for whoever is trying to help will create well-being, hope and upliftment for all souls and all forms in the material world.

Thank you

Let's align and harmonise with God's pure and unlimited mind and experience the same attitude of purest consciousness.

> *I am now with God,*
> *A mindset deep in the realm of light,*
> *Empty and full,*
> *Beyond the changing worlds,*
> *Beyond thought, yet, full of knowing,*
> *Beyond the need to act, experience and discover,*
> *Centred in the bliss of being,*
> *Constantly conscious,*
> *Constantly still,*
> *A mind full of love, empathy and compassion.*
> *Recipient of all prayers and sorrow-directed thoughts,*
> *Unaffected and holding nothing*
> *A love-centred compassion*
> *Knowing how each in their reach out to His supportive love,*
> *Receives the return according to their intention and their truth,*
> *Thus, God becomes the catalyst of all returns,*
> *Knowing all will be satisfied and all will be fulfilled,*

So, now He watches,
Observes,
And is still.

9

The End Game

In our connection with God, we reach our aim, the meeting, the reunification of the soul's long-lost relationship with God and the world of truth.

Now like an emerging flower beginning its role of fragrance and natural beauty, the empowered soul can become a channel and support for God's task of planetary renewal.

Yet, to discover and know such a being as God has been the aim of a few, often stated as impossible by many and not considered by most.
A Divinity seen or thought of as too far beyond man's ability to understand and experience.
All these positions have some validity and, at the same time, are entirely wrong.

Locked and trapped in the extreme depths of an impure and body-conscious mindset, it seems God is a long way off, an unapproachable purity. Being in such a state, the mind would probably be unable to think of and make such an approach.

Yet, I believe God is not an egotist, not one obsessed with His role and position. His being is benevolent and loving, an open door, yet, presents a way to His connection that is not that evident and yet, at the same time, is readily available.

For it is only through spiritual synchronicity is such a meeting possible. Through the use of our subtle intellect, we have the chance to come close and gain access to His direct power and unique being.

The actor has to leave the stage to change his costume. The freed soul becomes light and subtle and can then move to its desired connection of unity.

Just as a child is encouraged to walk and progress by its encouraging parent, God provides particular advice that the soul can take to arrive at this unity of support and empowerment safely.

Now more than ever, the soul will need faith in itself, its destiny and its connection with God. In front of it, it will have to stand and face alienation and increasing hostility and aggression from the old collapsing systems of a tired and degraded old world.

Never before on its spiritual journey has the soul faced such an overwhelming attack on its long-held and primarily imposed inner beliefs, for it has laid itself bare, it has shed its old-world masks and falsehoods, relinquished its old attachments and egoic attitudes, and so now stands honest and open, a heroic stance, a position of great courage. Still, in these nascent moments, it's also a position of significant vulnerability, especially from the opposing systems of materialistic consumerism and the ever-increasing negative beliefs of a very confused world.

This stance and assertion of spirituality would certainly not be possible without the help of God's love, who continually offers the soul His all-embracing power and cooperation to guide the mind through all the turmoil and turbulence of this change experience.
In surrendering to God's direct guidance, the mind receives the strength and courage to step away from its old attachments, fears and the entrapments of the illusory world of false and empty promises.

Our journey, destination, purpose, and beginning are all to this purpose- a discovery,

a reunion, a combining with the divine.
Like a spiritual sun, God illuminates and
transforms the lower worlds into universes of
light, each filled with beauty and radiance,
reflecting their unique forms of God-centred
light and the energy of the purest being.

Let's explore and experience further the
spiritual world of God:

> *A Supreme Consciousness*
> *Love-centred, light-centred,*
> *An awareness, constantly conscious*
> *Constantly constant,*
> *Compassionate and still,*
> *Benevolent in being, nature and form,*
> *Beyond change, beyond influence,*
> *Beyond the deteriorating world of*
> *matter,*
> *A doorway, an entry point,*
> *A pure form, a point form*
> *A vast ocean of absolute purity,*
> *Constantly full,*
> *Light form, love form,*
> *The Bestower,*
> *Silent and still,*
> *Not thinking, not seeing,*
> *Yet, seeing all,*
> *Aware,*
> *Far beyond*
> *Separate,*

Yet together, with all,
As one,
United in light, in energy,
In spiritual love,
Full of love.
So now let us reflect on this,
And experience the power of God's
infinite love.

The End

About the Brahma Kumaris

The Brahma Kumaris is a network of organisations in over 100 countries, with its spiritual headquarters in Mount Abu, Rajasthan, India. The University works at all levels of society for positive change.

Acknowledging the intrinsic worth and goodness of the inner self, the University teaches a practical method of meditation that helps people to cultivate their inner strengths and values. The University also offers courses and seminars in such topics as positive thinking, overcoming anger, stress relief and self-esteem, encouraging spirituality in daily life. This spiritual approach is also brought into healthcare, social work, education, prisons and other community settings.

The University's Academy in Mount Abu offers individuals from all backgrounds a variety of life-long learning opportunities to help them recognise their inherent qualities and abilities in order to make the most of their lives.

All courses and activities are offered free of charge. For more information:
www.brahmakumaris.org

For Brahma Kumaris publications

www.inspiredstillness.com
hello@inspiredstillness.com

Spiritual Headquarters
PO Box No 2, Mount Abu 307501, Rajasthan, India
Tel: (+91) 2974-238261 to 68
Fax: (+91) 2974-238883
E-mail: abu@bkivv.org

International Co-Ordinating Office & Regional Office for Europe and The Middle East
Global Co-operation House, 65-69 Pound Lane, London, NW10 2HH, UK
Tel: (+44) 20-8727-3350
Fax: (+44) 20-8727-3351
E-mail: london@brahmakumaris.org

Regional Offices Africa
Global Museum for a Better World, Maua Close off Parklands Road,
Westlands PO Box 123, Sarit Centre, Nairobi, Kenya
Tel: (+254) 20-374-3572
Fax: (+254) 20-374-3885
E-mail: nairobi@brahmakumaris.org

Russia, CIS and the Baltic Countries
Brahma Kumaris World Spiritual University
2, Lobachika, Bldg. No. 2 Moscow – 107140 RUSSIA
Tel: (+7): +7499 2646276
Fax: (+7) 495-261-3224

The Americas and The Caribbean
Global Harmony House, 46 S. Middle Neck Road,
Great Neck, NY 11021, USA
Tel: (+1) 516-773-0971
Fax: (+1) 516-773-0976
E-mail: newyork@brahmakumaris.org

Australia and Southeast Asia
181 First Ave, Five Dock, Sydney, 2046
Australia

Printed in Great Britain
by Amazon